I0843795

7 Days to End Anxiety and Phobias

Summary

Who am I?

My name is Thomas Beckham and I am a clinical psychologist. Over the past 20 years, I have worked with hundreds of people suffering from various forms of anxiety and phobias.

I have seen these issues and their effects on people's lives. I decided to write this mini guide to offer people suffering from anxiety and phobias a chance to take control of their lives and transform it.

I am convinced that, with this guide, people will be able to find a solution to their anxiety and phobias in just 7 days. My guide combines practical advice, proven techniques and authentic testimonies to help people face their fears and find the inner peace they deserve.

DISCLAIMER

The information provided in this mini-guide should not be considered as a treatment or replacement for professional treatment.

Readers should consult their doctor or other qualified health professional for any advice and medical treatment.

The authors and publisher disclaim any liability for the consequences that may result from the use of the information contained in this mini-guide.

The information provided is based on scientific research and professional knowledge and should not be considered as personal medical advice.

Introduction

Hello!

In this guide, you will learn how to overcome the fear and panic that often accompany anxiety disorder and phobias. We invite you to commit to following the steps of this program and to discover how you can take back control of your life.

The goal of this program is to help you feel more relaxed, secure and comfortable with your anxiety and phobias. It will help you find anxiety management methods and develop plans to reduce the symptoms and effects of phobias.

You will also learn to develop skills that will help you manage your anxiety and feel more comfortable in your environment.

We will discuss the main causes of anxiety and different types of phobias, and we will look at the role of perception and emotions in controlling anxiety symptoms. We will also teach you relaxation and breathing techniques to help you better manage anxiety and feel calmer and more secure.

We will also present strategies and tools to help you overcome your phobias and integrate them into your daily life. You will learn to manage your anxiety and phobias at every step of the process.

We will explain to you how to better understand your anxiety and phobias and we will offer you advice and practical strategies to help you overcome them. You will learn to analyze your reactions, confront your fears, and find solutions to your problems.

Finally, we will examine how to avoid relapses and how to live a more satisfying and fulfilling life.

If you commit to this program, you will discover how you can take back control of your life and learn to live with your anxiety and phobias. You will learn to recognize the causes and risk factors of anxiety and phobias, manage symptoms, develop positive skills and take preventive measures.

Finally, you will learn methods to find inner peace and well-being, learn to love yourself and give your life a new direction and a new meaning.

What is Anxiety and Phobias?

Anxiety and phobias are mental conditions that can affect your daily life and overall health. These disorders can manifest themselves in different ways and can be caused by environmental, biological, or psychological factors.

Anxiety is the general term to describe an emotional and physical reaction to an unknown situation, a threat or another source of stress. This can include a feeling of anxiety, fear, worry and anxiety, and a feeling of physical discomfort, such as stomach aches or sweating. Symptoms can vary in intensity and duration depending on the person and situation, and sometimes can be so intense that they interfere with functioning and quality of life.

Phobias are anxiety disorders characterized by intense, irrational fears of a specific thing or situation. Phobias can be divided into two main types: specific phobias and social phobias. Specific phobias are fears triggered by specific objects or animals, while social phobias are fears triggered by social situations, such as speaking in public or being observed by strangers.

The symptoms of anxiety and phobias can vary greatly and may include:

- Intense and persistent feelings of anxiety and panic

- Frequent headaches and stomach aches

- Heart palpitations and sweats

- A feeling of fear and insecurity

- Difficulty concentrating

- Frequent tiredness and insomnia

- An irrational fear of specific situations or objects

- Hypervigilance and difficulty relaxing

- Sleep Disorders

- Loss of appetite and nausea

- An uncontrollable urge to escape

- Difficulty making decisions

- Low self-esteem

In addition, anxiety and phobias can lead to irrational behaviors and attempts to flee or avoid. These behaviors can interfere with your ability to function in your daily life and to connect with others. People with anxiety and phobias may also develop a feeling of isolation and depression.

Why and How to End Anxiety and Phobias?

Anxiety and phobias can prevent you from reaching your goals and deprive you of the joys and happiness life has to offer. They can make you feel powerless and defenseless in the face of a situation that scares you. For those who suffer from it, it can be difficult to know what to do to find relief.

This guide is for anyone who wants to end anxiety and phobias. It is designed to help you manage your symptoms, take steps to improve your mental health and give you tools to cope with anxiety-provoking situations.

Here are 7 Steps to Help You Manage Anxiety and Phobias:

1. Understand the functioning of anxiety and phobias.

2. Identify your anxious thoughts and behaviors.

3. Learn to manage your emotions.

4. Learn to reduce your anxiety and develop strategies for dealing with anxious situations.

5. Develop skills to avoid the traps of anxiety and phobias.

6. Take measures to improve your mental health.

7. Prepare to cope with anxiety and phobias.

This guide will help you find relief and take back control of your life. It will guide you step-by-step and provide you with the tools you need to overcome your anxiety and phobias. You will learn how to identify the causes and symptoms of anxiety and phobias, how to manage your emotions, how to reduce your anxiety and develop strategies for coping with anxiety-provoking situations, and how to take steps to improve your mental health.

By following these steps, you will learn how to better understand and manage your anxiety and phobias. You will develop skills to avoid the traps of anxiety and phobias and take steps to improve your mental health. You will prepare to cope with anxiety and phobias and find relief and regain control of your life.

Tools and Strategies to be Discussed

In this guide, we will go in-depth on the tools and strategies to follow to overcome anxiety and phobias. We will start from the basics and guide you step by step.

We will cover self-observation techniques to help you become aware of your thoughts, emotions, and behaviors. You will learn to recognize and name your fears, understand their causes, and identify the situations in which they manifest. These techniques will help you identify and manage your anxiety-provoking thoughts and reduce their impact on your emotional state.

We will also look at stress management. You will learn to identify situations that make you stressed and to put strategies in place to cope with them. You will learn to manage your time and responsibilities, to face difficulties, and to accept that some problems cannot be solved. You will discover methods to better relax and to feel more relaxed in stressful situations.

Finally, we will focus on adaptive behaviors to help you adopt new attitudes and make more constructive decisions. You will learn to adopt positive habits and identify behaviors that are detrimental to your physical and mental health.

You will also be guided step-by-step through the change process. We will show you how to set up new strategies to approach anxious situations and we will discuss the important steps of the change process (preparation step, action step and consolidation step).

This book will also give you practical advice on nutrition and physical exercise. We will cover the basics of healthy eating and physical activity and you will learn to incorporate healthier habits into your daily life.

Finally, we will discuss relaxation and meditation techniques. You will learn to recognize symptoms caused by stress and use relaxation techniques to develop your calmness and concentration. We will also provide practical information on meditation and explain how it can be used to help you manage your emotions and take a step back from your anxious thoughts.

Day 1: Identifying Causes

The first day of your program to manage your anxiety and phobias is very important, as it will allow you to uncover the underlying causes of your issues. The causes can be numerous, ranging from genetic factors to traumatic events experienced in your childhood or more recent events that have triggered an anxious reaction. In order to find the causes of your anxiety and phobias, we will teach you to:

- Explore your memories to identify traumatic events.
- Identify the genetic factors that may be the cause of your anxiety and phobias.
- Understanding how negative thoughts and traumatic memories are linked to your anxiety and phobias.
- Discover current events and behaviors that may maintain your anxiety and phobias.

Understanding the causes of anxiety and phobias is essential in order to manage them. Once you understand the causes of your distress, you can then start to apply strategies to manage it. It is important to remember that anxiety and phobias are not a sign of weakness or lack of control: it is a normal process that can be managed. Therefore, do not feel ashamed, frightened or overwhelmed.

By exploring your memories and identifying traumatic events, you can start to understand what triggered your anxiety and phobias. It is also very useful to understand how your negative thoughts and memories are linked and can contribute to your distress. This can help you to identify current triggers and become aware of behaviors and situations that exacerbate your anxiety and phobias.

It is important to remember that it is normal to feel anxious or scared sometimes. However, if your symptoms are very intense, if you avoid situations because of your anxiety, and if you feel overwhelmed, then it may be time to seek help. There are many resources and programs that can help you understand and manage your anxiety and phobias.

What are the different symptoms associated with anxiety and phobias?

When you suffer from anxiety or phobias, you experience both physical and psychological symptoms, which can make life difficult. Anxiety and phobia symptoms can vary from person to person and can be more or less severe, but they all have one common presence.

Here are the most common symptoms related to anxiety and phobies:

- Nausea

- Dizziness

- Exhaustion

- Palpitations

- Shortness of breath

- Feelings of insecurity and vulnerability

- Difficulty staying calm and focused

- Increased Fear and Anxiety

- Panic Attacks

- Excessive Sweating

- Sleep Disorders

- Irrational fear of a specific object or situation

- Irrational Fear of Leaving Home

- Flashbacks

- Obsessive Thoughts

If you are experiencing any of these symptoms, it is essential to consult your doctor and discuss your concerns. He can help you assess the severity of your anxiety or phobia and find the best treatment for you.

It is also important to recognize that anxiety and phobias are often related. Someone suffering from anxiety may also suffer from phobias, and vice versa. If you are concerned about your anxiety, it can be helpful to consult a specialist who can help you determine if you are suffering from a phobia or generalized anxiety.

Finally, it is essential to understand that you are not alone in your battle against anxiety and phobias. There are many resources available to help you through this difficult time, including doctors, therapists, and support groups. You can also find comfort and support from your family and friends.

What are the possible causes of anxiety and phobias?

Possible causes of anxiety and phobia are numerous and varied. Some may be genetic and related to physical or mental factors, while others may be related to external events or triggering circumstances.

The main possible causes are:
Genetic and Biological Factors: People suffering from anxiety and phobia may have a genetic and biological history of anxiety disorders and other mental illnesses. Those who are genetically predisposed to the illness may be more likely to develop anxiety and phobia than those who do not have a genetic link.

Environmental Factors: Changes in the environment can also contribute to the development of anxiety and phobias. Traumatic events such as stress and abuse, as well as changes in the physical or social environment, can have an impact on the development and intensity of anxiety disorders.

Psychological factors: Psychological factors can also play a role in the development of anxiety and phobias. Mindset and beliefs can contribute to the way a person sees and handles certain situations and can even affect the intensity of their symptoms. People who have difficulty managing stress, making decisions, or expressing their feelings are more likely to develop symptoms of anxiety and phobia.

Behavioral Factors: Behaviors can also contribute to anxiety and phobias. People who are more inclined to avoid situations that might be anxiety-provoking can develop anxiety and phobia. Behaviors such as lack of physical activity, avoidance, and procrastination can worsen anxiety symptoms and phobias and can also contribute to their development.

In conclusion, genetic and biological, environmental, psychological, and behavioral factors can all play a role in the development of anxiety and phobias. Symptoms may be related to one or more of these factors. Understanding how these factors interact, then, can help individuals to better understand and manage their symptoms.

Learn to Identify and Understand Your Emotions

The first day of the mini guide 7 Days to End Anxiety & Phobias is dedicated to learning how to identify and understand your emotions. It is crucial to invest fully in this step if you want to get out of it sustainably.

Acknowledging and accepting one's own feelings can be a difficult step. However, it is the only way to move forward and manage your thoughts and reactions in an appropriate way.

The main emotions to recognize are fear, anger, sadness, surprise, disgust, and joy. Fear and anger are primary reactions and very common in response to anxiety and phobias, while sadness and surprise can also be felt.

Once these emotions are identified, further questions can be asked to learn more about their cause and effect. For example, you can ask yourself how strong the emotion is, or what it makes you feel.

It is necessary to understand the trigger or what triggers an emotion, whether it is negative or positive. Indeed, by having a deep knowledge of the things that stimulate or amplify an emotion, it is possible to use it to your advantage to better react to it.
A simple and effective way to understand your emotions is to describe them in a journal. It is advised to note the context in which you felt the emotion and what you were doing at the time. This will help you identify the situations that can trigger or amplify your emotions.

Finally, learning to identify and understand one's emotions is an essential part of the journey towards managing anxiety and phobias. Although this can often be a tricky step, it is possible to become familiar with one's emotions and to try to accept them. Using techniques such as meditation and developing self-compassion are effective ways to accept and manage them.

Day 2: Develop Confrontation Strategies

On the second day of our program to overcome anxiety and phobias, we focus on using tools and strategies to confront fears and anxieties. Developing coping strategies is an essential part of the healing process and can be very beneficial in helping to reduce stress and anxiety.

It is important to remember that not all strategies work for everyone and that strategies that work for one person may not work for another. Therefore, it is important to find the strategies that work best for you and incorporate them into your treatment plan.
Here are some useful conflict strategies:

- Practice deep breathing exercises or progressive muscle relaxation techniques to help reduce stress and calm yourself.

- Learning to focus on the present moment. This can help you better understand and manage anxious states.

- Try to find ways to counter negative thoughts with positive affirmations and more constructive thinking.

- Identify and modify behaviors that may be harmful.

- Learning to recognize and manage negative emotions and feelings.

- Focus on making informed and thoughtful decisions rather than making decisions on impulse or acting out of emotion.

- Find ways to support each other and talk to people who understand what you are going through.

- Demonstrate self-discipline and perseverance.

Using these strategies can be difficult and complex, and it can be useful to work with a therapist or specialist to help you find effective ways to use these strategies. It can also be useful to focus on self-awareness and stress and emotion management, and to strive to cultivate more patience, kindness, and compassion for oneself.

Learning to Better Manage Anxiety and Phobias

Day 2 being dedicated to developing strategies for dealing with anxiety and phobias, it's time to look at some methods that can help you better manage these situations.

Here are some recommended ways to help you better manage your anxiety and phobias:

- Becoming aware of your reactions: by recognizing the symptoms of your anxiety and phobias, you can better control them and find ways to lessen the negative effects they have on your life.

- Use deep breathing and relaxation: these relaxation techniques are known to be very effective for reducing stress and tension related to anxiety and phobias. By breathing more deeply and relaxing, you can reduce the level of anxiety and phobia and help you better manage these emotions.

- Use distraction techniques: by focusing on activities or tasks that help you distract yourself from anxiety and phobias, you can better manage them and avoid letting them take control of your life.

- Gradual Exposure: This method involves gradually exposing yourself to the situation or object that causes you anxiety or phobia. Starting with a low dose of exposure and gradually increasing the dose, you can learn to better manage your anxiety and phobias.

- Develop Positive Thoughts: By developing positive and constructive thoughts, you can better manage your anxiety and phobias and learn to accept your emotions.

- Seek Professional Help: if you find that your anxiety and phobias are taking over and you are not managing them as well as you would like, it can be very useful to get the help of a mental health professional to help you better manage these emotions.

In short, to better manage anxiety and phobias, there are many methods that can help you. It is important to take time to learn to recognize your reactions and develop methods to control and mitigate them, and to seek professional help if necessary.

Learning to Self-Encourage

On the second day, we will learn how to self-encourage. We will learn to recognize, appreciate and celebrate what we have achieved, which can be a really powerful resource to face anxiety and phobias.

Let's start by understanding how self-encouragement can improve our mental well-being and help us face our difficult fears. Self-encouragement is essential in helping us develop a more positive and constructive attitude towards difficult situations. Indeed, when we encourage ourselves, we are supporting and motivating ourselves to take positive action to face our obstacles and challenges.

For example, by praising ourselves for our hard work and discouraging ourselves less often, we can feel more confident and take more constructive steps to deal with difficulties. Furthermore, self-encouragement allows us to focus on the positives and to recognize our strengths and abilities.

Self-encouragement includes several components:

- We can thank and congratulate ourselves for the good times and the small achievements we have made, even if those achievements are not great.

- We can remind ourselves to let go and take a step back when we are faced with difficult moments.

- We can also remember to acknowledge and celebrate our strengths and resilience.

- We can also remind ourselves to take time out and do relaxing activities to help us to reground and unwind.

Finally, it is also important to remind ourselves that we can always choose to do things that make us feel good. This can involve activities that help us to relax, stimulate and support ourselves.

By applying these self-encouragement strategies, we can learn to encourage ourselves and take better care of ourselves. Self-encouragement can provide us with a source of confidence and support to confront anxiety and phobias and cope with any difficulties that may arise.

Adopt Healthy Habits and Behaviors

It is crucial to be aware of habits and behaviors that are good for your health and adopt healthy methods to face anxiety and phobias.

Gaining awareness. Gaining awareness of the habits and behaviors that you adopt to manage your anxiety and phobias is a crucial step. Some behaviors are good for your health and can be useful to face anxiety and phobias. Other methods can be harmful and help to maintain the vicious circle of anxiety and phobias.

Taking care of oneself. Taking care of oneself is very important to manage anxiety and phobias. This involves making sure to have a balanced diet and enough sleep, to do regular physical activity and activities to relax yourself.

Talking. Sharing your emotions and problems with trusted people can be extremely beneficial for both physical and mental health. Talking with friends and family members can help you better understand your emotions and give you different perspectives on the situation.

Avoid Unhealthy Behaviors. It is important to avoid any behavior that can harm you or make you more anxious or phobic. This can include the use of psychoactive substances, addiction to video games or the internet, excessive use of social media, etc.

Seek professional help. If you think you need extra help managing your anxiety and phobia symptoms, the safest option is to consult a mental health professional. They can help you to develop healthy coping strategies and to better understand and manage your emotions.

Day 3: Take a Step Back

On day 3 of our program, we invite you to take a step back from your anxiety and phobias. This means that we are going to help you to observe these feelings and reactions closely, in order to understand them more deeply. This will help you to gain access to a new level of understanding of these issues, as well as to find more appropriate solutions.

You can start by taking notes on the circumstances that were present before your anxiety attack or phobia episode. What were the factors that contributed to the emergence of your symptoms? What were your feelings at that time? What were your thoughts that were associated with it? Once you have captured this information, you can analyze it in more detail.

Then, you can take the time to examine and understand your adaptability and problem-solving processes. What helps you manage your anxiety and phobias? What tools and strategies have helped you through this situation? Lastly, what behaviors and reactions can you take to better manage your anxiety and phobias?

A good way to gain some perspective on your anxiety and phobias is to focus on the strengths and resources you have. What makes you strong and able to overcome your symptoms? What gives you the motivation and courage to continue on your journey towards a new mindset?

You can also take the time to assess your behaviors and reactions to your symptoms. What behaviors and reactions help you best manage your anxiety and phobias? What are the ones that are not appropriate and can worsen the situation?

Finally, take the time to reflect on your values and goals. What is important to you? What are you trying to achieve? What will enable you to lead a life you deem satisfactory? The answers to these questions will help you find the motivation and support you need to manage your anxiety and phobias.

Learning to Let Go

Learning to let go is an essential step to overcoming anxiety and phobias. Letting go means accepting and feeling comfortable with things as they are rather than desperately trying to change what one cannot change. This does not mean being passive, but rather having a more positive attitude towards life and learning to adapt to circumstances.

To learn to let go, there are several things you can do:

- Accept your feelings. That means accepting and recognizing that you are feeling fear, anxiety, or any other negative emotion. Don't fight your feelings and don't try to change them, but accept and understand them.

- Avoid worrying about what others think. You don't have to worry about what others think of you. This doesn't mean you should be rude or tactless but you should be comfortable with who you are and what you do.

- Learn to say no. If you constantly have others telling you what to do, you will waste your time trying to please them. Learn to say no when you are overwhelmed or don't want to do something.

- Making decisions. Don't keep putting decisions off. Take the time to think about what you want and make decisions that are good for you and can help you reach your goals.

- Take time for yourself. Don't try to do everything at once and learn to say no when you need to. Take time to relax and do activities that soothe you and that you enjoy.

- Don't be too hard on yourself. It is important to give yourself moments of break and not be too hard on yourself. Don't blame yourself for the things you didn't manage to do and don't compare yourself with other people.

- Have a positive attitude. Learn to accept things as they are and try to see the positive side of every situation. Don't focus on the negative aspects and try to see how you can make the best of every situation.

- Demonstrate patience. Learn to be more patient and don't expect everything to happen instantly. Patience is a virtue and it can help you to better manage anxiety and phobias.

In short, if you try to let go, you can learn to accept things as they are, to stop worrying about what others think, to say no when necessary, to make decisions, to take time for yourself, to not be too hard on yourself, to have a positive attitude, and to be patient.

Learn to Accept Yourself

On the Third Day of your stay towards the end of anxiety and phobias, you will need to learn to accept yourself. It will be highly beneficial for you to understand your limits and accept them. The negative thoughts you have about yourself are not the right ones and can have negative effects on your morale and wellbeing.

Therefore, you need to focus on how to practice self-acceptance and become aware of your limiting thoughts or beliefs. This will help you to give yourself a sense of freedom and power.

To achieve self-acceptance, here are some steps you can take:

Identify the thoughts that limit you.

Use positive affirmations to replace negative thoughts.

- Take the time to appreciate the small things in life.

- Learn to forgive, yourself and others.

- Accept your mistakes and learn to overcome them.

- Find ways to feel good about yourself.

- Exercise or do physical activities.

- Reward yourself for your efforts and progress.

- Tell yourself that you deserve happiness and love.

- Listen to your body and respond to its needs.

- Work on your self-esteem and confidence.

- Smile and laugh often.

- Love yourself and take care of yourself.

- Learn to respect yourself.

- Practice self-compassion.

- Focus on the positive.

- Speak of yourself with kindness and compassion.

By following these steps, you will learn to accept and welcome all of your feelings. You will start to see life from a different perspective. You will start to notice the small things that make life beautiful and you will learn to be more tolerant and understanding of yourself and others. This will lead to a healthier state of mind and a greater sense of happiness and satisfaction.

Learning to See Things from a Different Perspective

Have you ever felt overwhelmed by your anxieties and phobias? Have you ever felt like things were so bad that you couldn't cope? If so, then day 3 of your 7-day program against anxiety and phobias is made for you: learning to see things from a different perspective.

The first step towards a better understanding of what is happening is to identify the signs of stress or anxiety that manifest in yourself. What triggers your anxiety? What signs alert you that your anxiety is growing? What thoughts are you having? Taking the time to identify the signs and symptoms of your anxiety will allow you to better understand and thus better manage them.

Once you have identified the symptoms, it is time to start analyzing them. You need to recognize that, sometimes, anxiety can be overinvested and make you see things in a more alarming way than they really are. Taking a step back and looking at things in a more objective way will help you feel more at ease and better manage your stress and anxiety.

Start by examining the situation and try to set aside your biases and emotions to focus on the facts. You can also try to look at the situation from a different angle. Think about what would happen if you approached the same situation from another point of view. Study your feelings and thoughts from a more objective and rational perspective. This can help to put things into perspective and help you better understand what is going on.

You can also try to take a more positive attitude towards yourself and your anxiety. Try to look at things from a different perspective, seeing them as an opportunity to grow and learn. Approach things with an open and accepting attitude. Acknowledge that your anxiety and phobias are part of your life and that it doesn't necessarily have to be a source of stress.

Also try to remember that your anxiety and phobias are not an end in themselves. They can be overcome and you can learn to manage them. It's not about ignoring or pushing them away, but about accepting and understanding them.

Finally, learn to recognize the signs and means of reducing your anxiety and phobias. You can learn to use relaxation techniques, to indulge in recreational activities, to set realistic goals and to find support to help you. Use these tools to help you learn to see things from a different perspective and to better understand your anxieties and phobias.

Day 4: Show Confidence

On the fourth day we will look into ways to increase confidence and assurance. Self-confidence is the bedrock of any change and action, so it is essential to build a sense of self-confidence and to feel capable of pushing one's limits.

Let's start with the basics: to show confidence, you first need to build it. To do this, it's important to take time every day to reflect on your skills and abilities. Make a list of your strengths and talents and take the time to appreciate them. Also take the time to remember moments when you felt confident in yourself and your abilities.

Next, you need to learn to accept that you don't have control over everything and that's okay. Learn to open yourself up to new possibilities, to accept your mistakes and to accept compliments. This exercise will help you learn to accept your vulnerability and take the risks necessary to move forward.

Once you have built your confidence, you can display it. Here are some tips to help you do so:

- Be authentic. Be proud of your strengths and talents and show them to others.

- Take risks. Don't be afraid to make decisions or try new things.

- Stay positive. Don't let failures get you down and learn to focus on successes.

- Speak about yourself confidently. Use positive language and avoid comparing yourself to others.

- Take initiative. Don't wait to be asked to do something, take the initiative and achieve your goals.

Finally, it is important to continue cultivating your self-confidence. Take the time to practice and to feel capable of surpassing yourself. It is also very important to surround yourself with the right people and to receive support and motivation. Don't be afraid to ask for help and to confide your fears to the people you trust the most.

Develop Your Posture

Developing one's posture is one of the key elements in increasing one's confidence and releasing anxiety and phobias. To adopt a more determined and serene posture, it is necessary to practice staying consciously upright and to focus one's attention on the muscles of one's body.

Here's how to do it:

- Take the time to sit down and make yourself comfortable and relaxed. Take several deep and slow breaths, as if you were preparing to meditate.

- Focus on your body and imagine yourself as a stone statue. Make contact with the ground beneath your feet and sense the feeling of stability that results. Relax your hands and place them on your legs. Now, focus on your spine and visualize that your head is slightly drawn upward.

- Imagine your spine lengthening with each breath and standing tall and aware.

- Lift your shoulders and imagine that your arms are connected to your spine and they are stretching up.

- Avoid tensing up too much and keep a relaxed posture.

- Focus on your feelings and body sensation.

Once you have found your relaxed and upright posture, bring your attention to your diaphragm and take deep and slow breaths.

These simple and easy exercises will help you maintain a straighter and more serene posture. This will help you feel more clarity and have more confidence in yourself. A relaxed and conscious posture allows you to feel more secure and more centered. This can help you to face your anxieties and phobias and allow you to feel free and confident.

Learn to Speak More Confidently

One of the best ways to show confidence is to speak with more assurance. To do this, there are a few points to keep in mind:

- Use positive language: Remember that your attitude directly affects how your interlocutors perceive you. Use positive and encouraging language. Replace negative phrases such as I can't with positive affirmations such as I can.

- One of the simplest ways of speaking more confidently is to use the correct vocabulary and syntax. Avoid complex and jargon words and focus on simple and precise words.

- Use affirmations: Affirmations can be a very useful tool when you are trying to increase your confidence. Use short and concise phrases like I can do..., I can do it, I will make it, etc.

- Speak your mind: Don't be intimidated by others and dare to say what you think. If you disagree with something, don't be afraid to say so. This will help you show your confidence.

- Take breaks: One of the best ways to speak with more assurance is to take breaks between each sentence. This will give the impression that you have time to think about what you say and that you know where you're headed.

- Remember to smile: Don't forget that your attitude affects how your interlocutors perceive you. A smile can be a very effective way to show your confidence.

- Speak loudly and clearly: Another way to speak with more assurance is to speak loudly and clearly. This will give the impression that you're sure of yourself and that you know what you are saying.

- Show empathy: One of the best ways to talk in a more confident manner is to show empathy and respect towards your interlocutors. Listen to their point of view and show that you are listening.

- Listen carefully: A good practice to adopt when speaking to someone is to listen carefully to what they are saying. This will show that you are interested in what they have to say and that you are listening.

By applying these tips to your conversations, you will start to speak more confidently. If you want to go further, you can look for additional exercises and techniques online to further improve your confidence and learn to speak in a more confident manner.

Developing Self-Confidence

On the fourth day of your program to overcome anxiety and phobias you are invited to develop your self-confidence. To do this, you must surround yourself with positive people who encourage you to become the best version of yourself. You must therefore eliminate all toxic people from your circle and choose to surround yourself with friendly and positive people.

Next, you need to learn to accept your flaws and imperfections. Nobody is perfect, and that's okay. On the contrary, it's by recognizing one's limitations and accepting one's mistakes that one can learn and grow. Therefore, you need to learn to accept yourself and to love yourself as you are.

Moreover, you must learn to surround yourself with people who value you and encourage you to move forward. You must also find activities that make you feel good and give you confidence. It is also important to find activities that make you feel good and allow you to thrive.

Finally, to develop your self-confidence, you must learn to celebrate your successes and to congratulate yourself for every small step you take. You must also learn to congratulate yourself for your efforts and to celebrate even the smallest victories. You must learn to be proud of yourself and to recognize yourself for who you are.

To conclude, developing self-confidence is an essential step in overcoming anxiety and phobias. You must learn to accept your imperfections and to love yourself as you are. You must also surround yourself with people who encourage and support you. Finally, you must learn to celebrate your successes and to congratulate yourself for every small step you take.

Day 5: Identifying Your Own Values

Identifying Your Own Values, we will discuss and explore the values that are unique to us and that help us determine our beliefs and how we act. This will allow us to better understand what motivates us and drives us.

First of all, it is crucial to emphasize that the values we choose to prioritize in our lives give us a sense of purpose and enable us to move forward with more consistency. We are all different, which is why what we choose to value varies from person to person. Values can be taken into account to make decisions, guide our actions, or help us think about relationships.

Getting to know our values allows us to make informed choices. To better understand what our values are, here are some questions that can help us see more clearly:

- What is important to me?

- What motivates me?

- What makes me feel good?

- What are the things I would like to achieve?

- What gives me energy?

- What makes me feel accomplished?

Taking the time to answer these questions and maybe add some more can help identify our values and know what is important to us.

Once we have identified our values, it is important to be able to put them into practice. This will allow us to go towards our goals and to achieve what we wish. It will also allow us to give ourselves meaning and to learn to be in harmony with ourselves.

Finally, it is also important to take the time to put words to these values and to understand what it means for us. It is by being aware of our values that we will be able to apply them to our life.

Becoming aware of our values is an important step in better understanding who we are and what guides our choices. This step puts us in front of ourselves and allows us to get used to going in the direction of what motivates us. This will also help us better understand our needs and flourish.

What does my life mean to me?

Everyone has their own meaning of life. Discovering this meaning is essential for finding emotional and spiritual balance.

To identify one's own values, it is useful to ask oneself the following questions:

- What is important to me?

- What are my goals in life?

- What makes me happy?

- What gives me the energy and the motivation to move forward?

- What do I want to achieve in my life?

In order to progress, it is important to set goals for oneself and remind oneself every day what is important to them. One must also ask oneself what sets them apart from others, and focus on the aspects of their personality which make them unique.

Once we have identified our values, we can start to develop an action plan that will guide us towards a more fulfilling life. Here are some important steps to take to achieve our goal:

- Discover what is important to oneself and what motivates us.

- Reflect on what you really want to accomplish.

- Identify our strengths and weaknesses.

- Achieve our accomplishments and take time to celebrate them.

- Take risks and step out of your comfort zone.

- Set goals and achieve them.

- Identify and Avoid Negative Behaviors.

- Learning Chess.

- Practicing Gratitude.

- Rest and Relax.

Once one has identified their values and established an action plan, they can focus on enhancing their life. They can begin to look at things from a different perspective and view challenges from a new light. They can also learn to better listen to their body and allow themselves to rest and take time for themselves.

Finally, we must learn to accept our failures and see them as an opportunity for learning and personal growth. By learning to accept our mistakes, we can draw positive lessons and grow.

In summary, identifying values is essential to finding an emotional and spiritual balance. It is important to discover what is important to oneself, to reflect on what one really wants to achieve and to identify one's strengths and weaknesses in order to develop an action plan and reach one's goals. Finally, we must learn to accept our failures and to take positive lessons from them.

How can I set realistic goals?

Setting clear, achievable and feasible goals is an essential element to be successful in a project. It is paramount to clarify one's vision and goals to achieve satisfactory results.

First of all, it is essential to take the time to define what is important to you. To do this, it is recommended to reflect on your personal values and what really matters to you in life. Once these values have been defined, you can then direct your goals and achievements according to these values.

Then, it is wise to be precise and realistic when defining your goals. For this, you must approach the entire process step by step and not skip any steps. Precision and realism of the goals are essential, so take the time to properly define them.

Next, you must also set achievable goals within the given time frame. It is important to give your project a timeline in order to better organize yourself and monitor your progress. Short, medium and long-term objectives can help you follow your path and track your progress.

You can also use various organization and planning tools to help you set and achieve your goals. For example, you can use Excel spreadsheets, smartphone apps, or online tools to better organize your work and keep track of your progress.

Finally, don't forget to set goals that motivate you personally. When you set goals, it is important that they motivate you and make you want to achieve them. Otherwise, you will quickly lose track and your motivation.

In summary, identifying your own values and setting realistic goals is the key to successfully completing your project. Take the time to define your personal values, goals and the tools that will help you reach your goals on time and motivate you.

How can I find balance between my values and my actions?

It is essential to find a balance between your values and your actions. This can be difficult to do, but taking the time to reflect on what you consider important in life and what makes your life more fulfilling and meaningful is an important step in the healing process.

If you are having difficulty finding a balance between your values and your actions, here are some tips to help you:

- Take the time to reflect on what you consider to be important in life and what is important to you. Ask yourself questions like: What values matter most to me? What will make me the happiest and most fulfilled? What is my vision of life?

- Identify your short and long-term goals. Write them down to make them more concrete and to have a clear vision of your goals. You can even set yourself intermediate steps to help you achieve them.

- Ask yourself if your actions are aligned with your values. Regularly analyze what you do and ask yourself if your actions are consistent with your values. If you find that they are not, look for ways to correct the situation.

- Develop positive habits. Good habits can help you align yourself with your values and make healthier decisions. Try to find ways to incorporate into your routine things that give you pleasure and are in line with your values.

- Take time to reflect on the consequences of your actions. Ask yourself how your actions can affect your life and that of others. This can help you make healthier decisions and to find balance in your life.

- Set boundaries and stick to them. It is important to be firm on what is acceptable and what is not and to clearly verbalize those boundaries. Boundaries can help you align with your values and make healthier decisions.

- Learn to say no. Learning to say no is an important tool for finding balance between your values and your actions. If something does not align with your values, learn to say no and not to feel bad about it.

- Practice self-reflection. Take the time to think about your thoughts, feelings, and behaviors and look for ways to align with your values. Learn to listen to your intuition and make choices that are in line with your values.

- Listen to yourself. Take the time to listen to what your intuition tells you and what is most important to you.

Learn to trust yourself and make choices that are in line
with your values.

- Ask for help. Sometimes, it can be helpful to seek
professional help in finding balance between your
values and your actions. Surround yourself with people
that support and encourage you.

Day 6: Controlling Your Thoughts

Controlling thoughts is an important step in overcoming anxiety and phobias. In this section, we will examine the techniques you can use to take control of your thoughts. The first thing to understand is that you are able to control your thoughts. You can't control what happens, but you can control how you respond to it.

Controlling your thoughts means first learning to identify the negative thoughts that come and go in your mind. Once you have identified the source of your anxiety or fear, you can then work on developing strategies to neutralize your negative thoughts and replace them with more positive thoughts.

Here are some strategies you can use to control your thoughts:

- Identify your limiting beliefs: Take the time to identify if the thoughts that are limiting you are actually true. You may be telling yourself things like I can't do it, I'm not good enough, I can't succeed. Challenge these beliefs and replace them with more positive thoughts.

- Replace negative thoughts with positive thoughts: Once you have identified your negative thoughts, take the time to replace them with more positive and constructive thoughts. For example, if you think I can't do it, replace that thought with I can do it if I give myself the means.

- Create affirmations: Affirmations are positive statements that you can say out loud or write to help you feel better and take control of your thoughts. For example, you might say I am capable of dealing with this situation, I am stronger than my fears, I am capable of overcoming any challenges I face.

- Focus on the present: Another way to control your thoughts is to stay focused on the present. Focus on what is happening now and try not to project too far into the future or dwell too much in the past.

- Practice mindfulness: Mindfulness is a practice of focusing on the present moment and consciously paying attention to your thoughts and emotions. Mindfulness can help you to better understand your beliefs and develop new, more positive thoughts.

- Practice letting go: Letting go is another way to learn to better control your thoughts. This means that you should learn to accept certain things that you can't change and not to focus on what you can't control. Letting go can help to develop a more relaxed attitude towards life and its challenges.

Finally, remember that you can control your thoughts and it is up to you to decide which thoughts you want to keep and which thoughts you want to discard.

How can I recognize my faulty thoughts?

Misguided thoughts are beliefs that can be false or exaggerated. They create negative feelings and can influence how we interpret and react to things around us.

How can I recognize my wrong thoughts?

Here are some ways to recognize these thoughts:

- Questioning if the thought is logical: if the thoughts are not logical or realistic, it is possible that they are wrong.

- Knowing if thought is rational: a rational thought is based on facts and data, while erroneous thoughts are often exaggerated and can be based on prejudice or stereotypes.

- Questioning whether the thought is accurate and specific: mistaken thoughts are often vague and general.

- Knowing if thought is flexible and not rigid: wrong thoughts are often inflexible and do not take into account other points of view.

- Questioning if thought is short-term and long-term: erroneous thoughts can be short-term and not take into account the future.

- Wondering if thought is constructive: often erroneous thoughts are negative and destructive.

- Question one's own thinking: faulty thoughts are often based on a partial and biased viewpoint.

- Wonder if thinking is fixed: wrong thoughts are often too inflexible and cannot be changed, whereas rational thoughts can be changed according to information and events.

- Knowing if the thought is coherent: erroneous thoughts are often contradictory and do not align with one another.

- To wonder if thought is based on prejudices or stereotypes: erroneous thoughts are often based on prejudices or stereotypes and do not take into account differences and nuances.

By recognizing your erroneous thoughts and understanding their source, you can work on your beliefs in order to modify them so as to become more rational and flexible.

How can I replace my negative thoughts with more positive ones?

It is essential to replace negative thoughts with more positive ones in order to help manage anxiety and phobias. Fortunately, there are several ways to do this.

- Stay calm and practice deep breathing: Take the time to breathe deeply and slowly. This can help you to calm down and reduce stress and anxiety.

- Take the time to sit and reflect: Once you are calm, take the time to think about what is concerning you and what is the source of your negative thoughts. By precisely determining what is concerning you, you can better understand the source of your negative thoughts and decide how to remedy it.

- Use meditation and self-hypnosis to relax: Meditation and self-hypnosis can help you eliminate anxiety and phobias. Practice meditation and self-hypnosis exercises for several minutes each day. This can help you relax and better control your thoughts and emotions.

- Make positive affirmations and replace negative thoughts: Positive affirmations can help to replace negative thoughts. Focus on positive and encouraging phrases that you can repeat out loud. Positive affirmations can help to replace negative thoughts with more positive and constructive ones.

- Practice activities that make you feel good: Practicing activities that make you feel good and that give you a feeling of wellbeing can help to replace negative thoughts with more positive ones. Take the time to do activities that you like and that give you a feeling of satisfaction. You can also do things that help you feel calmer and more relaxed, such as reading, writing, gardening, listening to music, or taking a walk.

- Ask for help and seek support: Anxiety and phobias can be difficult to overcome. If you find that you need help to replace your negative thoughts with more positive thoughts, ask for help from a friend or a mental health professional. It can be helpful to talk to someone who understands what you are going through and who can provide you with useful advice and support.

How can I learn to better concentrate and relax?

Learning to better focus and relax can be very challenging, but with the right attitude and some techniques, it is possible to succeed. Here are some tips that will help you manage your anxiety and relax better:

- Set both short and long-term goals. Identify the goals you want to achieve and take the necessary steps to get there. Short-term goals will help you stay focused on the present and make faster, more efficient decisions.

- Increase your oxygen consumption. Take deep and slow breaths to oxygenate your body and calm your mind. This can help you feel more tranquil and better handle stressful situations.

- Reduce your consumption of coffee, tea, and energy drinks. Since these drinks contain stimulants, they can increase your anxiety and prevent you from relaxing.

- Take breaks. Don't be too hard on yourself and give yourself regular breaks. Taking a break can help you increase your concentration and better relax.

- Exercise regularly. Exercise can help reduce stress and better manage anxiety. Try to find a physical activity that suits you, whether it be swimming, running, walking or biking.

- Write down how you feel. Writing down your thoughts and feelings can help to clarify your ideas and better understand your emotions. You'll be able to focus better and relax if you take time to express yourself.

- Listen to relaxing music or sounds of nature. Music and sounds can help you relax and de-stress. Choose a music or sound that you like and listen to it when you start to feel stressed.

- Practice meditation. Meditation can be an excellent tool to soothe and relax yourself. It will help you refocus on the present moment, better manage your emotions, and better control your anxiety.

- Learn to relax. Take the time to relax every day. This can be done by practicing relaxation exercises, meditating, or listening to relaxing music.

- Try abdominal breathing. This breathing technique helps to improve concentration and reduce stress. Take a deep breath in through your nose and exhale through your mouth. Let your stomach fill with air and deflate with every breath.

- Practice mindfulness. Mindfulness is the art of being completely present and aware of what is happening around you. It can help you relax and better manage your anxiety.

- Take supplements. Some natural supplements can help you reduce your anxiety and manage stress.

Day 7: Expand Your Network

Day seven is the last day of this guide and, of course, it is just as important as the days prior. It is a day where you must take the time to reflect on all that you have accomplished thus far and put plans in place to continue your new journey.

This is the perfect time to develop your support system and social circle. During these 7 days, you have gained a new perspective on your anxiety and phobias. You have gotten to know yourself better and become aware of your strengths and weaknesses. You now know that you are able to face your anxiety and phobias and even overcome them.

It is thus time to find people with whom you can share your emotions and progress. You can do it in different ways:

Get to know people with similar interests to yours and who understand what you are going through. By creating new friendships with people who understand and encourage you, you will feel more relaxed and more confident.

Join online support groups or forums that deal with your anxiety and phobias. These groups and forums are places where you can ask questions and get answers from those who have been in your shoes and who are now free from their anxieties.
Find a therapist or therapy group to help you feel more comfortable and confident. Therapies can help you better understand and manage your emotions and find healthy ways of expressing them.

No matter how you choose to develop your support system and social circle, don't forget that it is an important step in your journey towards a sense of wellbeing and serenity. It is essential to find people who support and believe in you and encourage you to reach your goals.

In addition to finding new people, this is also a good time to reach out to people in your current circle who can be a great support. You can talk to them about your journey and ask for their help and advice to help you feel more at ease and to face your fears.

Day seven is the day of consolidating and strengthening your social support to help you reach your ultimate goal: to be free from your anxiety and phobias. Take the time to find people who will support you and who believe in you and your ability to reach your goal. Don't be afraid to develop new relationships and to take advantage of people who are already in your life.

What are the benefits of having a good support network?

Day 7 is devoted to building your support network. Having a good support network is essential for your physical and psychological well-being. The people in your circle can help you feel safe and secure and can be a great way to support you when you are going through tough times.

Here are some benefits of having a good support network:

- You have people to talk to when you need support. This means that you don't have to face difficult times alone. You can share your worries and difficulties with people who understand and can provide you with the support you need.

- You can also benefit from psychological support. People in your network can help you to face your difficulties and make informed decisions about what you should do.

- You also have access to emotional support whenever you need it. People in your network can give you advice and encouragement, help you to feel more secure and to feel more confident in yourself.

- You are more likely to find solutions to your problems and feel more relaxed when you have people to talk to who can understand and support you.

- You can also benefit from practical support, especially if you're going through a tough time. Members of your network can help you overcome the challenges you face and give you valuable advice and information.

Having a good support network can also help you feel more secure and in control of your life. People in your network can help you feel more comfortable and understand what you are going through.

Having a support network can also help you to feel more connected with your feelings and to better understand them. The people in your network can help you to become aware of your emotions and to accept them.

Having a good support network can also help you feel more comfortable in your relationships and communicate clearly and effectively with others. People in your network can help you feel more comfortable in your relationships and establish stronger connections with others.

In conclusion, having a good support network can be extremely beneficial for your physical and psychological well-being. People in your network can help you through tough times, better understand and accept your emotions, feel more secure and in control of your life. Furthermore, it can help you to build stronger connections with others and communicate effectively.

How can I strengthen my relationships with my loved ones?

It is essential to connect with those around us who are important to us. We must therefore take the time to strengthen relationships with our loved ones and maintain them. Here are some methods that can help us with this:

- Invite friends and family over to your house or to a restaurant. Take advantage of the opportunity to spend time together and catch up.

- Call and regularly listen to those you love. Inquire about their life and interests.

- Sharing moments together. It's important to find activities that you both enjoy. This could be a walk, a football match, a photo session or any other activity that suits you.

- Make plans together. Plan trips or vacations to spend time talking and having fun.

Once again, don't forget to communicate your emotions and thoughts. Sharing your feelings can help you feel more comfortable with your loved ones and to understand each other better.

Invite your friends and family to join in on online or group events (e.g., a game, a yoga class, a movie night).

- Exchange books, movies, and music with your loved ones.

- Learn to relax together. You can do yoga or meditation together, have a cup of tea or coffee and talk about your experiences and feelings.

- Find ways to have fun together. Play games, make jokes, and laugh.

- Ask for help when you need it. If you have difficulty taking care of yourself, reach out to family and friends for support.

- Share moments of reflection. Why not organize a discussion evening with a spiritual or philosophical topic?

- Let someone know that you are there for them. Don't forget to tell them that you are there for them and that they can count on you.

- Show kindness to others. Do small acts of kindness and let people around you know that you are there for them.

By strengthening our relationships with our loved ones, we can establish stronger and deeper connections, which can help us feel more secure and reduce stress and anxiety. Having emotional support can help us feel more grounded and make better decisions and take positive actions.

How can I make new friends?

Making new friends is essential for building your social circle and getting positive support. So why not try to make friends who can share your experiences and help you through tough times? Here are some tips for finding new friends and expanding your network:

- Go to events or meetings that interest you: you can find organized groups and clubs that match your interests. Talking to other people with the same passions as you can be very enriching and allow you to share your experiences.

- Take initiative and be open: even if you are shy and introverted, you can take initiative and open up to others. Invite your neighbors or colleagues for a cup of coffee and talk with them.

- Engage in social activities that you enjoy: the activity you choose will depend on your preferences and tastes. You can find groups that practice sports, cultural activities and more.

- Use social networks: Social networks are a good tool to make friends. You can join discussion groups, answer other people's posts and talk to them.

Be patient and persistent: don't expect it to be easy and don't be discouraged if you don't immediately find friends. Friendships take time and effort and require perseverance to develop.

In conclusion, having good mental health and positive support is absolutely necessary to counter anxiety and phobias. Making new friends can be an excellent way to gain support and a better quality of life. However, finding friends and establishing relationships doesn't happen overnight and requires patience and perseverance. By following the advice above, you can find friends who share your passions and help you face your difficulties.

Conclusion

This guide has been designed to help you manage your anxiety and phobias in just 7 days. We hope you have found the knowledge and tools you need to improve your quality of life and to feel more secure and confident.

The process of treating anxiety and phobias can be complex and take time. But it is possible to overcome it and be free from the symptoms that limit your life.

To succeed, you must be determined and find ways to manage your anxiety and phobias each day. Every day is a new opportunity to start, persevere, and make progress.

In order to maintain good mental health, here are some keys to overcoming anxiety and phobias:

Take the time to relax and do things you enjoy. Take time for yourself, for exercise, for a walk, for reading a book or simply for relaxation.

- Learn to manage your emotions and thoughts. Accept your emotions and recognize that you can handle them constructively. Learn to identify your thoughts and replace them with more positive thoughts.

- Be aware of your behaviors and how you react to stressful situations. Learn to ask yourself questions and take a step back to help you respond constructively to pressure and stress.

- Work on your self-esteem and confidence. Learn to accept your mistakes and be more forgiving towards yourself.

- Develop strategies to cope with your anxieties. Use relaxation techniques, cognitive and behavioral therapies, and breathing exercises to help you manage your anxiety and phobias.

- Don't forget to ask for help when you need it. Talk to a mental health professional and your loved ones. It is essential to find support and to feel heard.

- Know that you are capable of overcoming your anxieties and phobias. Remember that you have the power to make progress and regain your freedom.

By following these tips, you should be able to manage your anxiety and phobias and feel more fulfilled and confident in your life. We hope this guide has helped you find ways to feel better and more secure.

How can this guide help me?

The guide 7 Days to End Anxiety and Phobias has been designed to help you overcome anxiety and phobias that can hinder your well-being and productivity. It is rich in advice and practical tools that will help you understand, identify and manage your anxiety and phobias.

This guide is composed of advice and exercises that can help you find solutions to your emotional difficulties and improve your quality of life. It can also be used as a tool to learn to control and manage your anxiety and phobias in a positive and pro-active way.

Here are some of the things that this guide can help you do:

- Awareness of symptoms of anxiety and phobias and learning to manage them

- Develop skills to reduce your anxiety

- Discover relaxation techniques that can help you manage your anxiety and phobias

- Learn to manage your thoughts and emotions

- Take concrete steps to improve your mental health

- Finding effective ways to assert oneself and overcome fears

- Developing skills to stay calm and manage emotions

- Learning to manage anxiety and stress situations and confronting them constructively

- Understand the connection between thoughts and behaviors and learn to modify them

- Identify solutions for managing and overcoming your anxiety issues and phobias

- Discover healthy and positive ways to manage your anxiety and phobias

In summary, this guide is an excellent source of useful advice to help people suffering from anxiety and phobias to overcome them and improve their quality of life.

What are the next steps I can take?

At the end of this guide, you have acquired the knowledge and tools necessary to deal with your anxiety and phobias. The next steps you can take to ensure greater well-being and greater ability to face your future challenges are as follows:

- Learn to recognize your fears and confront them. One of the first steps to overcoming your phobias is to recognize and confront them. Analyze the reasons for your fears and take practical steps to minimize them.

- Find ways to manage your anxiety. Once you have identified your fears, you can try relaxation techniques to control your anxiety, such as deep breathing exercises, mindfulness exercises, visualization techniques, or meditation.

- Relax. Once you have found ways to manage your anxiety, try to practice relaxing activities. This can include reading, physical exercise, yoga or meditation, amongst others. Try to make sure you take time to relax each day.

- Talk to your loved ones. Find the person you feel closest to and talk to them about your fears and difficulties in facing them. Those who support you can help you feel more secure and to overcome your phobias.

- Find a healthcare professional. If you still can't get over your phobias and anxiety, you should contact a healthcare professional, such as a psychologist or psychiatrist, who can help you find the right treatments to help you face your challenges.

Thanks to this guide, you now have the basic tools to learn how to better manage your anxiety and face your fears. It is important to continue to make efforts and continue to practice using these tools to help you reach your goals.

Finally, be patient with yourself. Overcoming phobias and anxiety can take time and you may need to repeat exercises and techniques several times before you see results. Don't get discouraged and be kind to yourself.

Review and Celebrate Your Progress

At the end of this 7-day mini guide to overcoming anxiety and phobias, it is time to take stock and congratulate yourself on the progress made.

First of all, you must remember that each day you have made progress. Daily progress is underrated, but it is very important in finding inner peace. Every small step taken each day leads to healing and greater personal satisfaction.

Then, you must acknowledge and thank yourself for your courage and perseverance. Even if you haven't completely overcome your anxieties and phobias, you should be proud of your commitment to work on your mental health.

You also have to give yourself the right to bask in the feeling of satisfaction that you experience. Let yourself enjoy the euphoria and joy that comes with such success.

Finally, you must remember that you do not have to reach perfection. It is very important to set realistic goals for yourself and to remind yourself that healing and growth are a process that takes time. You must be patient and persistent and remember that every step is progress and moments to savor.

It is also important to have people you can talk to, who can listen and support you, and who will share in your joy. Find friends, mentors, professionals, and resources that can help you along your healing journey.

In conclusion, you should reflect on what you have learned and congratulate yourself for taking the first steps to a healthier and more satisfying life. You are halfway there and brave - congratulate yourself for your work and your determination to move forward.

www.ingramcontent.com/pod-product-compliance
Lightning Source LLC
Chambersburg PA
CBHW071059260726
48661CB00006B/2344